COOL THAT VOLCANO

PETER BLACK

CONTENTS

COOL THAT VOLCANO:

HOW TO HELP CHILDREN STAY CALM, MANAGE
ANGER AND MASTER EMOTIONS

By
PETER BLACK

FREE PRINTABLE POSTER TO HELP COOL THE VOLCANO!

At the back of the book is an opportunity to join the Peter Black mailing list.

As a reward for signing up to the mailing list, you will receive a free printable poster, linked to the techniques covered in this book, that you can use to help your children manage their emotions.

For N, my own little volcano...

INTRODUCTION

Children are wild these days, and they're out of control! That's the message we get from the news, from magazines, from television, from social media, and from society in general. I'm not sure I agree that children are wilder now than they used to be, but I do agree there is a problem with children and their emotions nowadays.

At some point, all children struggle to manage their emotions, some more than others. For some children, this means that they can become angry, can experience emotional outbursts, can be unreasonable, and can at times be downright frightening. These temper tantrums and emotional outbursts can have a negative impact on themselves, parents and guardians, siblings, pets, as well as some of the objects that may be thrown around or damaged in your home.

Perhaps you are experiencing difficulties with your child's temper at the moment, perhaps you are looking for help for the child of a friend or loved one. Whatever the case, and especially if you are the parent of a child who struggles with temper tantrums, I'll tell you one thing right now ...

It is very unlikely that you are solely to blame for your child's temper!

Sorry to go all bold on you there, but I think this is a crucial point to make. Children can struggle to understand and manage their feelings, and I know that as a parent the natural tendency might be to blame ourselves. Sure, there might be things that we could do better at those tricky points, or it might be that we have done things ourselves that our child has noticed and learned through watching that have contributed to their difficulties. But the chances that we are one hundred percent to blame for any difficulties our children are having in this area is quite unlikely.

The good news is that you can be a huge part of the solution. If you use this book as intended, I am confident that you will go a long way to helping your child understand what is happening to them, and how they can manage their feelings more effectively. I cannot guarantee that your child will never lose their temper again, or that they will never overreact in the face of some minor event; I'm not in the business of discussing magic wands. What I do have to offer in this book is a set of tried and tested techniques that can help your child make sense of what is happening to them more quickly, when those emotions begin to boil over. This earlier recognition will leave them much better placed to do something different and keep a lid on those pesky and more tricky feelings.

This book will also help you to teach your children about what to do with feelings, how to process them, as well as how to actually work through them in a calm and productive way. For too long in this country, the Victorian British 'stiff upper lip' has meant that some people have always been unsure when it comes to emotions. Feelings are a crucial and everyday part of the human condition. Now is the time we must start normalising emotions in our children and making it okay for them to talk about them without judgement, embarrassment, or shame. This book will assist you in helping your children make sense of what can feel like a veritable minefield for us as adults, never mind for them as they learn about a complicated world. Why should you listen to me? I think that is a fair question. I'm a parent myself, and whilst I'm not suggesting that I'm a perfect parent by any means, it does mean that I've had some of the experiences that you may be having at the moment. Have you experienced times when you just didn't know how to get through to your child, or times when you felt hugely confused by the massive overreaction being played out in front of you, feelings that caused embarrassment and shame when your child refused to calm down or listen to reason?

Aside from the above, my professional background in working psychologically with some very troubled individuals has helped me gather a great deal of experience and knowledge in the area of emotional management, particularly anger management. I have learned during my career that a few skills —and some basic emotional intelligence—can really help people who have had lifelong temper problems stay calmer and experience less stress and problems in their lives. This logic can apply to children too, and I have seen the positive results of teaching these skills to children myself.

Parents who have implemented some of the skills and information in this book have already begun to enjoy the benefits of calmer children, happier homes, and all round more peaceful existences. They have also been able to talk more openly with their children, in a language that everyone understands, meaning that potentially emotionally threatening situations have been avoided. These parents have also been able to develop a closer bond with their children, which has set the foundations for a lifelong emotionally rewarding relationship. You can have the same future with your children.

The people I have spoken to during my career so far, about the material contained in this book, have told me that the thing they were most surprised about was how simple it was to include these techniques and methods in their daily lives. They reported an almost immediate improvement in their own abilities to manage their feelings, and they highlighted how they have stayed calmer ever since. Of course, no one will ever be immune to losing their temper, and to tell you otherwise would be a lie. But, they have explained that it happens much less often, is less intense, and is much more likely to be easily and quickly managed, leading to fewer problems in their lives.

I promise that if you follow the steps in this book and discuss them with your children that you are much less likely to experience as many problematic situations because of your child, or children, and their temper. After this, you will experience a sense of increasing calm in your family home, and you will also feel that you are again in control, as parents should be. Furthermore, you will be able to enjoy a much closer bond with your children and develop a relationship where it is safe and possible for them to talk about their feelings.

Don't wait for a time when it feels that things have got completely out of control. If you think your child could do with more knowledge and skills in the area of staying on top of those tricky feelings, now is the time to act. Within this book, you will find the knowledge and the instructions about how to impart this knowledge to your children, so that you can start to turn things around and reduce the chances of feelings causing problems.

The emotional management information and skills you are about to learn will have a huge impact on your life. Each chapter will help you learn about how to help children take control of their feelings, rather than being controlled by their feelings. Take control of your children's emotional education now and embrace a more peaceful and happier life for all of your family.

HOW TO USE THIS BOOK

The first thing to say about this book is that it is aimed primarily at the parents of children who are aged between five and ten. The book is broken down into a number of different sections, all of which build on the knowledge and information that is included in the previous sections. The ultimate goal is to provide a framework and offer advice to help you discuss feelings with your children, identify practical ways that you can help them learn how to manage their feelings more effectively and help them to understand what is happening, and what they can do to keep things under control.

Broadly, there are four main sections in this book. The first section is focused on helping children understand emotions and how they function. It does this through the use of analogies, mainly that of the volcano. This section will help you to help your children make sense of what is happening at times when their feelings are getting increasingly intense. It will also help to normalise the emotional experience, so that they are comfortable with trying different ways of calming down. This first section also includes ways of helping children to feel motivated to stay calmer.

The second section is focused on ways that you can help your children to manage their emotions. This time, the analogy used is that of icebergs. These are the 'cooling' devices that your child can use to reduce the intensity of their emotions so they can make better choices and everyone can be less stressed! There are a wide variety of different techniques included in this section, and one of your main jobs at this point is to help work out which one works best for your child. Every child is different, which is why there is such a range of options here—trial and error is your best friend!

Section three is about how to help your children talk about and actually process their emotions, as opposed to either avoiding them or simply responding to them in an impulsive or explosive way. It looks at how to remove the sludgy lava that is left over after the volcano has cooled—this is used as a way of representing the problem that triggered the emotion. This part of the book will help you to teach your children how to express how they feel, as well as teach them about some of the things that can get in the way of emotional expression and make it more difficult for them to talk about their feelings.

Section four moves on to consider some of the things that you as parents or guardians can do to help children stay calm. What is your role more generally in keeping the volcano cool? It is something of a cliché to suggest that children are like sponges and pick up on everything around them, but this is true. What are they seeing in their immediate environment, and what are they learning about how to manage problems and what to do with their feelings. Also included in this section are issues such as triggers to emotional outbursts, and how the way you may respond to these incidents can serve to reinforce and cement a pattern of responding in your children.

So, now that we've covered what's going to be covered in the book, let's spend some time thinking about how the book will do it. The first thing to say is that this book is designed to help you talk to your children about emotions. There is only so far that 'doing things to' children will help them learn, especially when it comes to assisting them to employ skills to manage their emotions.

With this in mind, this book is designed to help you frame discussions with your children, the goal being that you will be able to explain these concepts to them, and they can be engaged in the process. Learning and improvement works better when those involved are collaboratively included. This approach is inherently more motivational, and it will help your children to learn they can be in charge of their feelings, rather than that relationship being the other way around. This book works better when it is used as a foundation manual for an interaction between you and your child, a process of active learning between the two of you that will leave all concerned better equipped to stay calm.

An important method used in this book is that of analogies. Emotions are complex and abstract concepts, even for us adults. This means that we need to find more simplistic ways of explaining them to children, which is where analogies can be extremely helpful. The main way this is achieved in this book is through the analogies of the volcano and the iceberg. This might all sound a bit unusual at the moment, but I can assure you that all will become very clear soon, and this will quickly set you on the road to tranquillity and effective emotional management.

There may be some references to research and statistics in this book. These are just meant to complement the content and help to reinforce the points being made. This is not an academic book, nor is it supposed to be a dry, statistical bore-fest! It is designed to be a useful *how to* guide, that will help give you the information you need to help your children remain calm and stay on top of their feelings. I've tried hard to keep the tone of the book light, yet informative.

So, let's not delay any more. It's time to start thinking about children and their emotions and how many children struggle to keep their feelings under control.

SECTION I:

UNDERSTANDING EMOTIONS

Chapters 1 – 6

ONE
UNDERSTANDING EMOTIONS

So, what are emotions? Well, the first thing to say is that they are a very normal part of being a human. In fact, they are a central part of the human condition, and without them, not only would life be incredibly dull, we would struggle to make decisions on a daily basis. Whilst we all like to view ourselves as rational and balanced individuals who always use our heads rather than our hearts, this is not the case, nor is it desirable. Emotions are crucial in decision making. You are probably familiar with the idea of *acting on your gut*, and this is how emotions play a role in our decision making.

All of us have feelings, and they are generally a force for good and can complement our lives in many positive ways. This is even true of emotions that are generally considered to be negative, such as anger. Sir Bob Geldof got angry about famine in Africa, and this led to worldwide efforts to address the problems there in the guise of *Live Aid*. We should therefore not fear feelings (even negative ones), as they are part of the rich tapestry of life. Instead, we should celebrate and enjoy emotions and teach our children to do the same.

The goal in this book is not emotional repression, or refusal to acknowledge or accept that emotions are present or exist. Rather, the goal is to help our children learn to safely and calmly understand and process their emotions, before talking about the things that have contributed to troublesome feelings.

Think about a time when you really lost your temper, when perhaps you totally overreacted and ended up doing something that you later really regretted or are perhaps now ashamed of. Now think about how hard you found it in the moment to stay calm, to make a more rational and less damaging decision. Now remember that you're an adult, and even you found it difficult with all of your experiences and knowledge of the world. Children have to manage their emotions without these skills or experiences. They are expected to *know* they should be doing better and can at times be punished for failing to stay calm or making a better choice at a time of emotional stress. My goal here is not to make you feel guilty, nor is it to judge you for punishing a child who failed to stay calm; I'm simply trying to evoke a bit of empathy for the child in your life who needs help in learning how to manage emotions better.

There are a number of reasons that children can struggle to manage their emotions, and below is just a few of these reasons:

Poor impulse control - Children are still learning about how to manage their feelings and desires, meaning that often if they want something, they just do it, without the benefit of any self-control which would allow them to think through the reasons why doing what they want in a situation can be problematic. Think about the child who just takes someone else's ball and then blows his top when his parents admonish him for it.

Poor problem solving - Children don't always have the reasoning skills to think a problem through all the way to its logical, rational, and fair conclusion. This means that they often take shortcuts and act in ways that are more likely to lead them to experience some emotional difficulties in the process.

Struggling with delayed gratification - Generally, children are terrible at being patient and delaying gratification, even if it means that they miss out on even greater rewards. There was a very famous experiment in which children were asked to sit in front of a single marshmallow. They were told that if they were successful in not eating the marshmallow for a set period of time, they would be allowed to eat two marshmallows. As you might expect, they generally couldn't wait for the increased reward. Essentially, telling a child that they have to wait is never a fun activity and can be met with surprising levels of frustration and anger.

Negotiation - This is a process that children do not tend to be very skilled at. They are often susceptible to bribery, as I'm sure we all know. However, they are partial to the odd mini explosion when their efforts to negotiate with us are met with a steadfast and consistent 'no.' When these efforts fail, frustration is often not far behind.

Poor communication with adults - Children do not have all of the verbal skills and abilities that adults have. This means that even if they know what they want or fully understand what they would like to do, they cannot always transfer this knowledge to adults very successfully. They might not know what words to use, or how to explain whatever is troubling them, and this can lead to an increase in the intensity of their emotions.

Meeting expectations - Children don't always know how to respond or behave in situations that can often be novel and brand new to them. This means that they can sometimes do the wrong thing, or they can easily misinterpret the actions and behaviour of others. This can lead to them doing things that can mean they end up in a heightened emotional state.

Self-soothing - Children cannot always calm themselves down independently. This is especially true if they have been brought up in an environment where people around them do not try to manage their emotions. This difficulty means that during times of emotional stress, they can find it impossible to put those emotions back in the box and respond in a more helpful way.

Hopefully, this will help you to feel reassured that all children will at times struggle to manage their emotions, and that many will engage in difficult behaviour because of this. According to the National Institute of Mental Health, 36% of children throw a tantrum in the presence of an adult that is not their parent(s). Just over a quarter of children (28%) have broken or damaged objects as a result of their difficulties in managing emotions. Again, about a quarter of children (26%) have been reported to have blown up as a result of reasons unknown (seemingly losing their temper for mysterious reasons), and 26% of parents reported being concerned about the length of time that the loss of emotional control lasted. Finally, 24% of children have bitten, hit, or kicked another person. As you can see, the chances that you are alone in having a child who struggles to understand and manage their emotions is very low indeed.

So, how do we explain all of this to children? As we are going to be talking to the children about thinking about themselves as volcanos, it might be worth thinking about thoughts, emotions, and feelings, as *lava*. Therefore, in the next chapter, we will start to consider how this lava can lead to problems if it is not understood and processed properly.

TWO
CHILDREN ARE LIKE VOLCANOS

Children are like volcanos. Well, we all are really, but at the moment, we're focusing on the children. How are they like volcanos? Well, when volcanos heat up to a given temperature that is too high to contain the lava, they explode and erupt, spewing hot and destructive lava all over the place. When children are not successful in calming themselves, they become *hotter* and *hotter*, until there is an emotional outburst (an eruption, if you will). It is these outbursts that we are trying to teach them to control and minimise. Please remember that this is not the same as ignoring or supressing the emotion; rather, it is ensuring there is a greater chance of allowing children to calmly process the emotion.

So, we've established that we are all like volcanos. The key difference, though, is that adults are normally better controlled volcanos who have built-in cooling systems that help to stifle the rising lava. Adults have lifetimes of experiences and an ability to use consequential thinking to help convince themselves that calming down and not having an award-winning paddy is probably the best way forward. Most adults have learned skills and strategies to help them stave off temper and to much more quickly return to a calm state of equilibrium.

Children are unregulated volcanos. This is where you come in as adults. The rest of this book is going to help you learn more about why the volcano erupts, and what you can do to initially be volcano coolers—before handing the icebergs over to the children—and help them learn how to be their own emotional police. Emotional management and calming down is a skill, and like any other skills, it needs attention, practice, and reinforcement. These are the steps that are going to make your children expert volcano coolers.

THREE
WHEN VOLCANOS ERUPT

In this chapter, we will look at the reasons why emotions can become difficult to control. So, why do volcanos erupt? In scientific terms, real volcanos erupt as a result of the increasing temperature of the lava inside, which continues to heat to the point where it cannot be contained any more, and it bursts out of the top.

In humans (of all ages), the process is similar. In terms of the analogy that we've been using, the lava (thoughts and feelings) begin to heat up because of a triggering event (we'll get to those later). The thoughts and feelings (lava) then become increasingly hot and intense to the point of an emotional outburst (eruption).

The process that is going on underneath all of this is the changing level of what is technically called *emotional arousal*. The basic theory is that we all function on an arousal curve and that to operate at our optimum, we need to maintain our level of emotional arousal somewhere in the middle. If our level of emotional arousal is too low, we will perform poorly, probably because we will be lethargic and apathetic (as can often be the case with feelings of depression). Essentially, the volcano is dormant, and the complete lack of lava that is heating up means that nothing gets done. However, if our level of emotional arousal is too high, we will again perform poorly. In this case, it is because we will be overheated, which means that we won't think things through, we will respond too rashly, and we will make poor choices. The volcano has become superheated and erupted and hot lava is spewing everywhere with no regard for the damage being caused.

Therefore, the basic theory behind effective emotional management is to keep our level of emotional arousal at the optimum level (in the mid-range). This means that if it increases too much, we need to use techniques to bring it back down to the middle. This helps us make sure we don't do anything we regret. This is what we need to teach children to do.

What happens if we don't teach children how to cool down their volcanos? Well, if we do nothing, and they don't learn how to do this, they can end up erupting quite often. This can be unsettling for the children themselves and for those around them. Emotional explosions and eruptions can be stressful for all involved, and so it is important that we help children learn how to cool their volcanos down.

When the volcano erupts, people can be upset by what they see and experience. Humans are social animals, which means that we all have a huge impact on each other. When we see someone we care about upset, for whatever reason, we can end up internalising some of that, and we can also end up feeling upset. Our moods impact on each other; therefore, we have a responsibility to do what we can to ensure we are not harming others by not working hard to keep on top of our emotions. We also have a responsibility to help the children in our lives learn these skills too.

If people don't learn how to manage their emotions, the result can be damage to people and things around us. We all have that friend or associate who can't manage their temper and ends up throwing things around, or ends up shooting their mouth off and embarrassing themselves and others around them. They can cause physical and emotional harm, and this, whilst it can be difficult, is avoidable. Exploding volcanos can also lead to objects being damaged, and it will probably only be a matter of time before an emotional management failure leads to a precious belonging being damaged beyond repair.

I was reminded recently of a fable which I think makes the point about the damage anger can cause, so I'll share this with you now.

A young girl continues to lose her temper and becomes angry. Her mother, running out of ideas of how to tame her, tells her that for every day she becomes angry, she should hammer a nail into a post in the garden. After a year, there are many nails in the post. The daughter makes the observation that on some days she did not have to put a nail in the post, and her mother agrees. Her mother says, 'Now, every day you are not angry, you can take a nail out of the post.' After a number of months, the post has fewer nails in it. One day, the two of them are in the garden together. The girl is pleased that the post has less nails in it, but she observes that now there are a lot of holes in the post. Her mother tells her that the holes represent the lasting damage that has been caused by her anger, and that this is also true for people.

Emotional eruptions can damage those around us in a long-term way, and remembering this can be a big help in cooling the volcano down. This is one of the things we need to help children understand.

FOUR
HELPING CHILDREN UNDERSTAND
THE VOLCANO

So, let's take stock of where we've got to. We've talked a bit about how emotions function, and what can go wrong when they're not managed very well. We've talked about some of the reasons that children can often find it hard to manage and express their emotions appropriately and some of the reasons that they might lose control in the first place. We've covered a few basic concepts, and I've introduced you to some of the analogies that you can use that will help children to understand what is happening to them, and ultimately, what they can do to prevent those eruptions. This chapter is going to focus on how we help children understand the concepts that have been covered so far, because without this understanding, they're going to struggle to stay on top of those difficult feelings.

Let's recap. This is what we've covered so far:

Volcano – This is a way of thinking about themselves. A healthy and functional volcano stays at a medium temperature and gradually releases lava in a productive way when it needs to.

Lava – This is a way of describing the thoughts and feelings that are inside the volcano/child. If these feelings become too hot, the volcano erupts.

Eruption – This is what happens when the lava has become too hot and has come spilling out of the volcano, potentially leading to harmful consequences. This is the part of the process we are trying to help children minimise.

So, now that we're all clear on what has been covered so far, we need to find a way of helping our children understand these concepts. In the spirit of open communication, which is very much a founding principle of this book, this can only really be done through talking to your children. As adults, we need to be role models for our children, and ultimately, we want to be at a point where our children feel able to talk openly about how they're feeling, and now is as good as any other time to start talking to each other. It sounds corny, but it really is good to talk, and it is something that I don't think happens enough between people, including us adults and our children.

If children feel they're being included in the process, and things are being worked out collaboratively, they are much more likely to be inclined to try things out. Do you remember how you felt when you were left out of decisions, whether it was at work or in a social setting? It sucks, and it leaves us feeling fairly put out. No one likes to feel they are having things done 'to' them. We are much more likely to be motivated to actively engage in the process if it is something that we feel included in and that things are being done 'with' us. This is also true for children who already have limited control over so many other areas of their lives.

People have different learning styles, so again this will apply to your children. Do they understand things better through written words, conversations, or pictures? You probably know your children better than anyone; so use your knowledge of them to try to work out which approach will work best.

How have you explained things to them in the past? What have you noticed that they learned more quickly and what did they seem to take a bit longer to get their head round? Investing a bit of time in working this out will help you pick the approach you think is likely to be most successful. Don't worry if you don't make the right choice here, you can always go back and try another approach.

The most important thing is that you keep trying until you are confident that the child 'gets' it. Without this knowledge being securely understood, it is going to be difficult for them to understand the rest of the techniques to stay calm and talk things through. Don't forget that you are unlikely to be the only adults in your child's life. What has your partner noticed? or grandparents, uncles, aunts, and extended family? Your child's current teacher is likely to be an excellent source of information at this point too, as someone who spends all day trying to teach your child different concepts and information, they are likely to be very knowledgeable in the kind of approach that might work best with your child.

If your child is good with language and understands quite abstract concepts, then it will probably work just fine to talk the analogy through. You might want to draw a simple flow chart as you are talking through it together, and you could put it on the bedroom wall or in a different accessible area of your home as a visual reminder of what you have talked through together. The trick is just to introduce one concept at a time and don't over-load your child. Attention spans are not great at these ages, and we need to keep it interesting, engaging, and even fun. If they enjoy the process of learning about the volcano, they will be less resistant to it and much more likely to learn quickly.

If your child is a visual learner, then it might be that images and pictures are going to be your chosen tool to help explain. You could draw a volcano, explain the concept along with that of lava and eruptions, and then either stick that on to a blown-up photograph of your child (in their tummy area), or simply draw a rough sketch of your child around that of the volcano. You could involve your child in the artsy parts of this process; this will help keep them engaged and enjoying it. If you wanted to get really fancy, you could draw lava coming out of their mouths or shooting out of their hands and feet to represent the damaging hot lava that can result from overheated volcanos! If you do choose this more visual approach, don't forget to get them to talk about it as they do it—it's supposed to be fun, but it's also focused on what you want them to learn from the process.

One thing to keep in mind is that children are likely to need some examples. So, once you have established all the elements of the analogy with them so far, try to help them identify some examples. You might find yourself saying something like 'Do you remember last week when I had to take away your Xbox, because you had been rude to me, and you ended up angry and upset and hit your sister because she was laughing? When that happened, your volcano got too hot, and it ended up erupting.' This will help them to really make the links between their real lives and the volcano analogy. For bonus points, get them to see if they can independently identify times when the volcano recently erupted. You will need to be quite sensitive at this point. Children can be ashamed of getting into trouble or hurting people they care about. We are not on a mission to induce guilt or shame; we just want them to be able to recognise when the volcano did get out of control, so they can make sense of the analogy.

All children are different, and you know them better than anyone else. This means that you are likely to know, or at least be able to have a good guess, about the method and pace of your explanation at this point. You may need to split it into parts and do it over a few days, or you may be able to get it all explained and understood in one sitting. As I already mentioned, don't panic if you feel it didn't go as well as it could have at this point. Perhaps you can leave it for a few days and then go back to try a different technique. Learning how to best explain these issues to your children is already helping to open up those lines of communication that are going to be so important moving forward.

FIVE

PROBLEMS CAUSED BY ERUPTING VOLCANOS

This chapter is going to focus on some of the things that can go wrong as a result of poor emotional management. So, what can go wrong when the volcano erupts and that damaging lava spills everywhere? This chapter will explore these problems, as well as the importance of helping children understand the damaging consequences that unregulated eruptions can have, as a first step to helping them develop motivation to keep the volcano cool. The consequences can be about feelings, objects, and our relationships, so it is important that we help children to understand that if they don't try to manage their emotions, they can inadvertently cause harm to others.

Now that we've established that talking to children about what can go wrong when they do not try to manage their emotions is important, we need to spend some time thinking about how we are going to approach this. Children are sensitive souls at the best of times, so we need to be quite careful and gentle in the way we talk about these issues. The goal of this particular discussion is not to encourage or try to install negative feelings in our children but simply to help them understand that it is important to try to manage their emotions and highlight some of the problems that might occur if they struggle to do this on a consistent basis.

So, what are some of the costs of not keeping the volcano cool that we can talk to our children about? Below are some of the issues you may wish to discuss with your children. Of course, as always, you know your children better than anyone does, and you may wish to discuss some extra issues that are relevant to your lives specifically. Also, you will be able to use real examples from your lives that will help to illustrate the points you are trying to cover. Here are some general points to consider discussing:

Bad feelings - It can be quite upsetting to lose your temper, and afterwards, there can often be a period of regret and other negative feelings. These feelings can be particularly unhelpful as the presence of negative emotions can contribute to a downward spiral that can make difficulties worse and can impact on levels of confidence and self-esteem that children experience. We all know as adults that when we think back on times in our lives when we blew our tops and ended up causing a scene or saying things we regret, we can often feel very embarrassed, even when these events were many years ago. If this is how we can end up feeling, then the same can be true for children. These feelings of embarrassment can lead to a reluctance to talk about problems; none of us want to talk about things that have left us feeling ashamed or embarrassed. Sadness and guilt can also be present after the volcano has erupted and children see that they have upset people they care about.

Damage - Losing control of our temper can cause damage in a number of different ways, and we need to help children understand what some of this damage can do. For example, it is important that children understand that letting the volcano erupt without trying to intervene means that sometimes they might want to get rid of the lava by punching, biting, or kicking, and that this type of behaviour can be very harmful—not only because of the physical pain that is caused, but also because of the emotional harm that can be caused. It is the emotional harm that children are less likely to understand, so this is a key point to help our children comprehend. It's not just people that can be harmed; it is useful to explain that erupting volcanos might target objects that are within arm's reach. I'm sure we all know that person who regularly has to replace console pads or electrical items that have not performed as they should have and have been launched against a wall or across a room.

If children are particularly expressive in how they deal with their emotions, it might be the family pet that bears the brunt of their frustrations. Animals and humans are not the same. (I'm sure you've already noticed this). Children may not always understand that because pets don't always reject or avoid them after being subjected to an emotional outburst, this doesn't mean that what has happened was not harmful or that the consequences will not manifest in a different way at some point in the future. Relationships can be negatively impacted on because of poor emotional management, so we need to help our children understand that friendships can be jeopardised, or at least damaged, by them not always being able to keep their volcanos cool and under control. Through discussions, we can help our children understand that regularly spewing hot lava all over their friends is not likely to cement or strengthen these friendships.

Conflict - As well as causing problems in relationships that already exist, those who struggle to manage their emotions are much more likely to experience regular conflicts with people they interact with. As described above, struggling to manage emotions can lead to poor choices and difficulties in working through problems with other people, which in turn can exacerbate problems with keeping the volcano cool. Simply put, if you struggle to keep a lid on it, you are going to struggle that little bit more with getting on with people in this world, and given that humans are social animals, that is going to cause problems throughout your life.

So, what have we learned in this chapter? We need to help children to understand the potential negative consequences that can occur when they don't keep their volcanos cool, or that have already been apparent as a result of their tempers flaring up. We need them to understand that not managing emotions can lead to further problems and will not help them to solve whatever problem or frustration is flummoxing them. However, we need to have this discussion in a sensitive and gentle way. We're not trying to make our children feel terrible and like bad people. We're just trying to gently make the point that erupting lava is damaging. In the next chapter, we'll spend some time helping them to understand that not only can this damage be avoided, but that by keeping the volcano cool there is a whole set of positive consequences that can be enjoyed.

SIX

MOTIVATING THE VOLCANO TO STAY COOL

So, how can we motivate our volcanos to keep their cool? Psychological research tells us that positive reinforcement works much better than punishment, and it is much more likely to lead to an increase in the types of behaviour we want to see. In this instance, that is improved emotional management.

This means that one of the simplest ways of reducing negative emotional management strategies is to hugely reinforce times when your children do well in how they manage their emotions. Rewards (which can often simply be verbal reinforcement) will be hugely powerful for the child, and it will encourage them to try their best the next time they're in a difficult situation. Everyone likes a pat on the back (even if they say they don't), and children are no different. They will work hard to earn your praise and rewards. We'll get to this in more detail later in Chapter 18.

This chapter deals with some ways in which you can help your child to 'buy into' the benefits of keeping the volcano cool. As humans, whilst we like to think of ourselves as altruistic cherubs who do lots of lovely things because we are just wonderful people, realistically, this is unlikely to be the case. Sure, we do things because we can be nice, but a lot of the time we do things because there is a benefit to us in doing it, and whilst that may not be the only reason we do things, even fringe benefits can be a powerful incentive that encourage us to do good things. This is also going to be true for children. So, part of our job is to motivate them to keep their volcanos cool, and below are a number of things we can talk about with them in order to leave them feeling more inclined and motivated to try out some of the techniques discussed later in this book.

Good feelings - Managing our feelings in difficult situations can be very rewarding, as can being someone who is considered skilled at this more generally. If children are able to keep the volcano cool, and this is noticed and reinforced by the adults around them, they can experience a range of positive feelings, such as pride and excitement, and these types of positive feelings are very powerful reinforcers, as most adults will attest to.

School - We all know how important this part of our lives is, yet it happens at the point of our lives when we are the least equipped to deal with it! Anyway, school can be a testing environment for the best of us, and most children want to do as well as their academic abilities allow, whether that is to please their teachers, us, or just because they are naturally motivated children. One thing that can be significantly disruptive to learning though, is a child's inability to stay calm in the classroom environment. Therefore, one benefit to discuss with your children is the idea that if they can keep the volcano cool, they are much more likely to succeed when it comes to learning, not least because they can actually concentrate on what is being taught, as opposed to erupting all over the place.

Role-modelling - A lot of children will' have other, younger children in their lives, such as siblings or cousins. Children can feel very rewarded by thinking of themselves as having grown up responsibilities, as being a good role-model, and as someone that younger people can look up to, and it is a great way of selling the idea of effective emotional management to children. If they understand that other children will watch and learn from them, they might want to make sure they're doing everything they can to keep the volcano cool.

Friendships - In the formative years, children are learning how to attain and maintain friendships with other people. Indeed, at this point in life, friendships feel very important, and I'm sure you've already had experiences with children who are distraught because they have fallen out with friends for one reason for another. One reason that children can fall out with each other is poor emotional management. There is an opportunity to talk to children about how keeping the volcano cool will mean that they are less unpredictable, and this will make it easier for others to be friends with them. We all know what it's like to have someone in our lives who can just explode for apparently no reason. Spending time with that person can be stressful and hard work. We don't want to feel like we're walking on egg shells, because others cannot manage their feelings. The same applies to children.

Good choices - We have discussed earlier in this book about how our level of *emotional arousal*, or how hot the volcano is, will directly impact on the types of decisions we make, and how much quality there is to our thinking. We know that the hotter the volcano, the lower quality our decision making is going to be. We need to help our children understand this relationship. We want them to understand that they need to keep their volcanos cool so they can make good choices. This success will become self-evident as they begin to observe that their good choices become successful in a compounded way, just like consistently bad choices can snowball into much bigger problems than originally existed. We can help our children understand that keeping the volcano cool is central to this process.

Bullying avoidance - One of the sad facts of life is the extent of bullying that exists in the world. It is an evil cancerous pastime and one that needs to be tackled head on, rather than ignored or swept under the carpet. It's probably impossible for children to get through school without ever experiencing bullying, or situations in which other children are unkind to them. One thing that can make children vulnerable to bullying is the ability to be *wound up*. I know as a child that it was very entertaining to wind someone up and watch the rocket go off. Often, the person who ends up getting into trouble is the one who has blown their top, as opposed to the person who caused the problem. We all know those wind up merchants who just love to load the gun and pass it to someone else to fire. We need to help our children ensure they are not accepting these 'loaded guns.' If your child can keep their volcano cool more often than not, they are going to offer very limited entertainment to other children. Bullies are then more likely to move on and try their luck on some other unfortunate child.

So, what are the key points of this chapter? Basically, we all do things, because we see some underlying benefit to doing them (to others, but primarily to ourselves). The above is just a short list of what I consider to be several of the likely many key benefits to keeping the volcano cool. You will know your child better than me, so you might just want to pick a few that apply most meaningfully to your child. You may be able to think of a few more that will be really empowering and motivational for your child. Everyone wants your child to keep their volcano cool, including your child themselves. It's your job to sell it to them in a way that leaves them feeling extremely clear about what is in it for them.

SECTION II:

MANAGING EMOTIONS

Chapters 7 – 9

SEVEN

DETECTING A RUMBLING VOLCANO

In section one of this book, we covered some of the basics of emotions and emotional management. We also explored some of the reasons why poor emotional management can be so damaging and how we can try to motivate our children to work hard to keep on top of their feelings and keep the volcano cool. We also covered some of the main ways that you can have these discussions with your children.

Section two of this book is going to focus on the actual nuts and bolts of emotional management for your children. How can children tell that the volcano is superheating? What tools can they use to try to cool things down and stop the potentially harmful descent towards eruptions? These are the issues we are going to start exploring now.

When we humans begin to experience an increase in our level of *emotional arousal*, this is accompanied by a set of what can be referred to as physical cues. These physical cues are basically physiological reactions from our body that indicate that we are experiencing a change in our level of emotional arousal. These physical cues can come in many different forms, and we will all experience different cues at the point we become angry (or whichever emotion is relevant).

Another way of thinking about these physical cues is to think about our basic human reactions. You will probably be familiar with the *fight or flight* concept. This relates to times when we are in situations where our safety is at risk. During these times, this fight or flight reaction gets us ready for just that—either to stand and defend ourselves through fighting or running away and trying to find safety. You may be able to recall times when you've been in these types of difficult situations. It might be that you heard really bad news, felt scared about what was happening, or sensed danger for some other reason. What you might have noticed during these times were your physical cues. You may have noticed 'butterflies' in your stomach—this is your body temporarily shutting down your digestive system, as digesting that meal you've just eaten is not going to be a priority if you have to sprint away from danger. It might have been a dry mouth you noticed—again, you won't need to swallow in a fight, so your body slows down saliva production.

How do we explain this to children? Well, at this point, we can return to our volcano analogy. We have discussed how physical cues tell us that we are undergoing a change in our emotional arousal. So, to use the analogy, we can liken this process to the shaking and rumbling of a volcano as the lava inside it begins to heat up as part of the process of building up towards an eruption.

Why is it helpful to be able to notice when the volcano is rumbling? Well, put simply, noticing this allows us to intervene. If we notice that we are starting to bubble over, then we can take steps and do things to prevent an eruption. So, if we teach children to notice when they are rumbling, then they can use some of the techniques we are going to explore soon to make sure that the rumbling doesn't escalate into full blown eruptions. It is also important that children learn to do this themselves. Whilst we as adults can help with this process (and this will be crucial initially), we are not always going to be there when the volcano starts to rumble; the independent ability to manage their feelings is one of the greatest gifts we can give our children.

So, what are these physical cues that we've been talking about? Below is a list of things that can occur in our bodies that might tell us that the volcano is rumbling, and that we need to do something to stop the process and avoid a potentially damaging eruption:

- Shaking
- Changes in temperature (hot/cold flushes)
- Tensing of muscles (could be specific areas - e.g. shoulders)
- Dry mouth
- Reddening around the face and neck
- Butterflies in the stomach area
- Clenched fists or teeth
- Changes in facial expression
- Changes in pitch/tone/volume of voice
- Changes in heart rate (normally speeding up)

THE ABOVE IS NOT an exhaustive list of physical cues, but these are probably amongst some of the main ways that we might detect that our emotional arousal is changing, and that we need to do something to interrupt the procession towards a loss of emotional control. We probably know ourselves which of these physical cues manifest in us when we are under emotional stress, but how do we help children understand their own physical cues? As with the rest of this book, discussion is your best friend here.

Talk to your children about what they notice happens in their bodies when the volcano starts to rumble. Perhaps a change in their facial expression is a dead giveaway; perhaps they go a bit red around the face. You will have made some observations yourself about what happens to your little volcanos at these times, and you can discuss your observations with your child. See if they recognise these cues in themselves. Try to make a list with them of the things they notice. It might only have two or three things on it, but that's fine. It's much better to have a shorter list of these volcano rumbling detection clues that are actually meaningful, as opposed to a big long list of inaccurate red herrings.

Once you have a bit of a list that you have put together with your child, why not place it somewhere in your house where you can refer to it at times you need to. You might want to take a picture on your smartphone as well so that you can easily refer to it once you are out and about. You can then use this as part of helping your children understand what is happening to them, by getting them to point at which 'rumbling clue' is being experienced. It is important to think about the learning styles that were discussed in Chapter 4. It might be that your child works better with pictures for their list, rather than written words. Try to adapt the approach you use to discuss this to best suit your child.

In summary, we all experience physical cues at points when there is a significant change in our level of emotional arousal. These physical cues can be described as rumbling clues that tell us the volcano is moving closer to eruption. We can help our children identify which rumbling clues they are experiencing, and we can use this knowledge to help them begin to regularly recognise the times when the volcano needs to be cooled down. For this part of the process, they will need an iceberg. And that is what we will be moving on to in the next chapter.

EIGHT
USING ICEBERGS TO COOL VOLCANOS

In the previous chapter, we spent some time talking about the clues that might tell us that the volcano is starting to rumble and that the lava is warming up on its way to a potential eruption. We've talked about things to look out for and what this might mean for the little volcanos in your life.

So, what now? Well, now that we know what to look out for, we now know when we need to intervene. This is a process that we as adults are likely to be heavily involved in initially, before we can reduce the extent of our involvement and hopefully hand more or less all control for volcano cooling over to the child. There would be little point in teaching children about what the clues are that the volcano is rumbling, if we were not going to spend time teaching them and encouraging them to practice the techniques to actually intervene and cool the volcano.

This chapter is going to focus on the different techniques that you can teach your children to help them cool their volcano down. These techniques, or interventions, are the tricks of the trade in terms of emotional management. These are the actual things that your children can do in order to reduce their level of emotional arousal and ensure that they don't do things that they will regret later and that will cause problems.

Thinking about our analogy, we are going to refer to these intervention and techniques as icebergs. That might sound a bit unusual initially, but if you think about it, it actually makes a lot of sense. When the volcano starts to rumble and the lava inside is heating up, popping an iceberg into the mouth of the volcano is a great way of cooling it down. The iceberg will melt and cool the volcano, and by the time the ice has melted completely, the volcano should be dormant again, and the child in your life will be ready to make sense of what has happened and talk things through with you. In the next chapter, we're going to spend some time talking about the different types of iceberg that exist, and you can introduce your child to them so they can learn how to independently cool down their volcano.

So, how do we introduce the concept of the volcano-cooling iceberg to our children? If you cast your mind back to Chapter 4, we discussed ways of discussing these types of concepts with your children. Remember, no one is likely to know your child better than you, so you probably know how your children learn best. It might be that they learn best through pictures, or it might be that they understand things better through demonstrations, or it might be that straightforward talking is the way to get through to your child.

Once you have decided how to introduce and discuss the various icebergs available to your child, you may need to spend some time thinking about how you're going to keep these icebergs in the minds of your children. Again, it might be worth placing a list of the icebergs somewhere where it can be referred to by both yourself and your child. This list can just include words, it might include pictures, or it might contain a combination of the two. You could, if you were feeling particularly creative, take photographs of your child executing each of the icebergs and use this as part of your list. This is quite a fun approach, and research is clear that children learn better when they're having fun, something which I'm sure is also true of us adults.

What you might observe as your child starts to use the various icebergs is that it looks like they don't work. Don't panic! This is a process of trial and error, and that means that your child needs to keep trying different icebergs until they find the one that works best for them. It might be that not every iceberg works for every situation. For example, at times when children feel that they are in a direct conflict situation, they may not want to take some deep breaths; they may want to squeeze a pillow instead.

Children are like us, they need to experience things and try them out before they can start to develop an understanding and increased levels of confidence in using the icebergs. It might be that they need to use certain icebergs a number of times before they learn how to use them properly—practice makes perfect! Another thing to consider is that they may need to use a combination of icebergs to cool their volcano. There are no hard and fast rules about this; you just need to help your child find what works for them. The secret is not to give up, and to continually encourage your child. If they see you giving up on the icebergs, it will be no time at all before they follow suit, and then you're back to square one.

What have we covered in this chapter? We have highlighted the fact that icebergs are a crucial tool to help children cool down their volcanos. We have reminded ourselves that we need to think carefully about how best to introduce the topic and discuss it with our children, bearing in mind what we covered earlier in the book about learning styles. Luckily, there is a good range of icebergs to try and they are covered in the next chapter. This is particularly helpful as there now needs to be a process of trial and error where you might be trying a few different icebergs, or combinations of icebergs, to find out which ones suit your children best, or perhaps help in certain types of situations most effectively. The next chapter will cover the nuts and bolts of volcano cooling (emotional management), so let's get down to business!

NINE

TYPES OF ICEBERGS

Now that we have been introduced to the concept of the cooling iceberg—which can be used to prevent volcanos erupting—let's have a look at some of the different icebergs that exist that we can help our children practice. We've discussed how to use the concept of the iceberg, and now we need to think about some of the different types of icebergs that are available. Let's not forget, one of the overarching principles of this book is that you know your child better than anyone else, so you will have some good ideas about which of the following icebergs will suit them best. And remember, there is no need to panic if the ones you start off trying don't turn out to be that helpful, as you can always try other ones. That is the main reason that there is quite a selection of different types of icebergs to choose from:

Going to a safe place - This might sound a bit like a *time out*, and in some ways there are similarities. However, there are also key differences. Time out on *the naughty step* is normally somewhere where the adult tells the child they are going. This technique is different as your child can make their own decision to go to their safe place (tepees or internal play tents are good for this) to have some time away from the conflict or trigger that they feel is contributing to their volcano beginning to rumble. You, as the adult, can of course also suggest the child does this, but it should feel like a collaborative decision, as opposed to a child having their autonomy and own ability to independently manage their feelings overridden. This is likely to be more of a home-based technique, so if it is used in isolation, it may not be that effective. Being in this safe place allows the child a bit of time and space away so that they can re-process what is happening and start to talk themselves through the reasons to be calmer.

Having a safe item - This is similar to the safe place concept but is much more portable, meaning that it has the benefit of being available to be used anywhere geographically. This is similar to having a comforter, something that will help children to feel calmer, and it essentially frees up their mind so they can concentrate on doing the thinking that will help the lava temperature to drop, so they can cool their thinking and feel calmer.

Breathing techniques - Never underestimate the power of breathing. It's something we all take for granted and something that we barely pay attention to. Yet, we really should think more about it. At times, our emotions may get stronger or out of control. Stopping for a second or two and taking some deep breaths can really interrupt our brain and body's ability to allow our thoughts to race, and we are forced to take a literal moment away from the internal escalation. The great thing about this technique is that it is totally free, and it can be used anywhere. Children might feel a bit self-conscious about doing this, so they can always be encouraged to walk somewhere out of sight and take some deep breaths. This process will help to clear their mind and allow them to focus on more helpful ways of evaluating the situation that triggered the volcano to start rumbling, and it may encourage them to take these steps in the future to reduce the chances of an eruption occurring.

Count to ten - This is a great technique that can be used in isolation or one that can be used directly after a child has decided to use the deep breathing technique described above. It is as simple as it sounds—the child simply counts to ten. This can be done out loud or internally in the child's mind. Initially at least, it might be better to encourage your child to count to ten out loud, just so you can be confident that they are going all the way to ten. This might sound like a pedantic and insignificant point, but it does matter. If your child is not going all the way to ten, they may be tempted to stop early, and this means they are not accessing all of the calming opportunities and time that they will get if they count all the way to ten. You can always count with them until they get used to the technique. Again, this is free, accessible everywhere, and really effective.

Hugs - This is quite a straightforward technique, and one that I probably don't need to explain in a huge amount of detail. Sometimes, when you can see that the volcano is rumbling and there may be trouble ahead, stopping for a moment and offering a hug will take the wind out of their sails and cool their volcano down instantly. If a child sees a way out of a conflict, they might be tempted to take it. The interesting thing about this technique is that it often relies on the adult being willing to offer a hug, and if you also feel riled by your child's behaviour, or whatever is happening at the time, this can be a difficult thing to feel motivated to do. However, a hug is clearly going to feel reassuring and safe, and it could be just the bit of safety and reassurance that your little volcano needs to help them find a bit of space and time to do things differently.

Pillow squeeze - Sometimes the volcano has got too

close to an eruption, and the only way of being able to move on to some of the cooling techniques is to discharge some of the pent-up frustration. This might normally be done by someone getting hit or something flying across the room. Instead, this iceberg is about finding a safe object to squeeze in order to use up some of the frustration that has built up. This can be an item that has been mutually agreed upon, and a pillow is an excellent choice. We don't want anything selected that is remotely human looking—using this as something to squeeze at times of frustration could inadvertently reinforce unhelpful ideas about taking frustrations out on people. Again, you might suggest to a child that they could go and give their pillow a squeeze, or they might make this decision independently.

Going for a walk - This one is going to be most practical if you have some time on your hands. A bit of fresh air and some time away from the trigger should help to allow for a bit of time and perspective to help the volcano cool. Again, try to make it as collaborative as possible. There might be some local areas that your child enjoys visiting, and if they are able to choose one of these places to walk to, then they are more likely to feel empowered and, therefore, implicitly more motivated to try their best to keep their volcano under control. This really is the crux—you've probably spotted the theme. Giving your child options and an ability to make independent choices is what is going to leave them feeling skilled and empowered. As a lot of emotional stress is caused by feeling out of control, then having a big say in how they go about resolving the situation will be hugely helpful.

Contact with a friend - Sometimes, all we need is a good chat with someone important in our lives, and that can help us calm down and see the situation from a different perspective. Friends are important to children, and we know how often they will listen to them (even often ignoring our wise words, much to our chagrin). This means that if your child is struggling to cool the volcano independently, it might be that a friend can help. If you think about how adults give something up or change problematic behaviour, such as giving up alcohol, they are likely to use the support of a group, or perhaps they might even have a *sponsor* or a *buddy*. Why not identify a child who can act as a buddy for your child and could be telephoned when your child is struggling with their temper. You may want to discuss this with the buddy's parents, to make sure that they are comfortable with the arrangement. You may also need to ensure that the selected buddy is someone who is going be helpful. This person needs to be a role model who can help to cool the volcano down, rather than adding further heat to the already-boiling lava! This might sound like quite a lot of pressure for a child, but a buddy isn't expected to counsel your child and teach them emotion regulation. If anything, they are most likely to be helpful as a positive distraction, just to take some of the sting out of the situation.

There's a lot of techniques to remember here, especially in the heat of the moment. Don't panic though; there are ways of managing this. One way to do this is to have a list on the wall, preferably with some images that your child can point at to help you understand which iceberg they think will help at that point in time. This list, or set of images should be in an accessible place to all of the family, so its usefulness can be maximised. Don't worry if art is not your thing, there is a free printable poster available to you at the back of this book, as a thank you for buying the book. Just print it out and stick it on the wall and you have a handy guide ready to go straight away.

So, there we have it. Above are eight different icebergs that can be used to cool the volcano. As described in the previous chapter, not all of these are going to work for your child. Part of your role in teaching these techniques to your child is to help them navigate the process of trial and error that will be necessary to work out which icebergs suit them and their personality best. Don't panic if the first few don't work, there are others to try, and it might be that it is just a bit of practice that is needed before these icebergs really start to make a difference.

SECTION III:

PROCESSING EMOTIONS

Chapters 10 – 12

TEN

WHAT'S WRONG WITH A DIRTY VOLCANO?

Okay, so what have we covered in this book so far? Well, we've discussed what emotions are and how they function. We've talked about how, if they are not managed carefully, they can often lead to the volcano erupting and leading to further problems. We've also covered the types of iceberg that we can help our children to use in order to interrupt the heating of the lava and cool down enough to lead to better decisions. Section three of this book is focused on helping children learn how to effectively process and discuss their feelings, as well as make sense of what is happening to them in terms of their emotions.

This chapter, specifically, is focused on some of the problems that can be caused by not processing emotions. What can go wrong if children struggle to process their emotions or intervene at points they are close to erupting? This chapter will have a look at some of the problems that can be caused if they remain unable to process, make sense of, and discuss their emotions after they have managed them. This is an important topic in the broader sense of emotional management, as the skills that children can learn about keeping the volcano cool can assist them into adulthood, and can ensure that they do not suffer the consequences of long-term pent-up negative emotions.

We have previously talked about lava being a useful way of describing thoughts. We know that as the lava/thinking heats up, we know that the volcano is getting closer and closer to an eruption. We all know that if an iceberg is inserted into the volcano, it will melt and cool the lava. This is very helpful, and it helps to buy time to increase the chances that good choices will be made. However, after an iceberg has helped to cool the volcano and positive choices have been made, sometimes there can still be some residual upset or grievances in the volcano, and this can be considered to be a result of the remaining *sludge*, which is effectively lava that has been cooled but remains in the volcano.

Therefore, the next stage in effective and safe volcano management is teaching children how to remove sludgy lava. I'm sure you can think back to times when you were full of sludgy lava yourselves. It might have been a time when you managed to avoid conflict and resolved a situation, but you still felt upset or a bit unhappy about what happened. This sense of unease or ongoing residual negative emotion—and this can feel really unpleasant—is in itself a problem. There are other problems that can be caused by residual sludgy lava as well.

Reduced tolerance to triggers - When we have gone through a difficult situation and have experienced an increase in our level of emotional arousal, we can be quite worn out, and we can feel strained. This is a period of time when our emotional batteries are recharging, things are reducing back to the mid-point, and we are settling down to normal again. This is quite a tricky time for us insofar as our tolerance is reduced. This means that it does not take much for us to be tested again, and if we are not careful, even the smallest comment can lead to eruptions that on other days would be very unlikely to occur. This is therefore more likely to lead to a future conflict.

Missed learning opportunities - If children do not have the opportunity to discharge any residual emotional angst, then they won't learn what to do when they are in this position in the future. This means that the discomfort of not knowing how to deal with increased levels of emotional arousal, post hoc, will be repeated in the future. Just as helpful coping experiences can be positively reinforced, poor coping experiences and strategies can be reinforced too. Over time, if volcanos don't get to empty their sludge helpfully, then the chances that they will not do this again next time they need to is increased. If this pattern is consistently reinforced, then the difficulties may remain into adulthood.

Containment and 'bottling up' - I'm sure we've all heard the expression *to bottle things up*. Well, this is what can happen if the sludge is not dealt with appropriately. If the sludge is not removed properly from the volcano, then it will just get added to every time there is an eruption, or even a near eruption, and over the time this happens, the resilience and tolerance to triggers is reduced. If children do not learn how to remove their sludgy lava, then all we are doing is teaching them containment. Don't get me wrong, containment is better than unmanaged volcanic eruptions. However, we are striving for better here, which is why we don't want to settle for containment, we are working towards emotional processing. The rest of this part of the book will help with this.

Relationship difficulties - For those of us who have a significant other in our lives, we know what it's like if there have been problems that have not been properly processed or talked through. This can contribute to tension in the relationship, which can in turn leave both parties vulnerable to further emotional discomfort and disruption. This can also be the case in friendships and professional working relationships, so not talking things through is rarely a recipe for success.

Brooding and urges for revenge - Not processing emotions in a meaningful and thorough way can leave residual sludgy lava that festers, and this can lead to ongoing thoughts that are not helpful. If we do not take the time to properly clean out the volcano and remove all vestiges of sludgy lava, then it just decays, and this can lead to unhelpful thinking. Sometimes, for some people, this can lead to thoughts of revenge. Some people can think that the only way to remove sludgy lava is to propel it out by doing something to *even the score*, even if the situation has been resolved on a superficial level, and even if the volcano has been cooled with a well-placed iceberg.

So, as you can see, a dirty volcano is a problem. That's why the third part of this book is focused on processing emotion and removing sludgy lava. In this chapter, we have looked at why dirty volcanos are potentially damaging and some of the specific problems they can cause. In the next chapter, we are going to spend some time looking at some of the benefits of learning how to process emotions and how keeping volcanos clean can be hugely helpful in a number of ways.

ELEVEN
REASONS TO KEEP THE VOLCANO CLEAN

We've spent some time looking at the problems with having a dirty volcano and how it can cause difficulties in a number of different ways. This chapter moves things on, and we'll spend some time looking at the benefits of having a clean volcano and how this can improve life for those who can achieve this (and this, of course, includes our children). You might be wondering why this stuff is important. The thing is, as we discussed earlier, in order to sell an idea to someone, we need to be able to let them know what's in it for them. Therefore, if we need to convince others of what can be helpful about improved volcano management, particularly in terms of cleaning the volcano, we need to know what the benefits are for us. This is what we're going to spend some time talking about in this chapter.

There are many really important benefits for keeping the volcano clean:

Meaningful problem resolution - If the volcano is clean and well organised, the chances are that when conflicts arise they are going to be resolved in a genuine way. It also means that children are well set to cool the volcano quickly should they find themselves in a tricky spot again sometime soon. If the volcano is cleaned properly and thoroughly, it does not leave room for simmering resentment or any urges for revenge—this means that there is a reduced chance of an eruption down the line.

Improved relationships - Cleaning out the volcano can help improve relationships in a number of ways. Firstly, it helps children to learn the crucial skills of emotional expression and talking problems through. This is essential in adult intimate relationships and will stand them in good stead to work through hard times and difficult situations with other people in their futures. Also, it helps your child learn about ways of talking about difficult topics, and this can also be helpful in improving and strengthening bonds with partners in adulthood and family and friends in childhood. You can also learn more about your child, and they will learn more about you. That will also assist your child in adulthood.

Increased tolerance and resilience - We have discussed several times that the better people become at keeping their volcanos clean, the more resilient they become at managing triggers which might get the volcano rumbling. A key part of this process is the cleaning of the volcano. Once you have got through the process of cleaning out the volcano several times, you become less vulnerable to your volcano moving beyond a rumble towards a full blown eruption. Being resilient in terms of emotional management, and less likely to respond unhelpfully to triggers, is clearly a desirable goal.

Improved perspective taking and empathy skills - Part of cleaning the volcano out means that children are encouraged to think about situations from the perspectives of other people. The more they do this, as with any other skill, the better they will get at it, and this will also help them greatly as adults. Furthermore, learning how to think about situations from the perspective of other people assists us in using the skill of empathy. If children can learn about empathy from a young age, often the volcano will be even easier to cool, as they will be able to think ahead to interrupt the rumbling volcano before it needs to erupt.

Encouraging calm - Sometimes just the act of processing emotions and cleaning out the volcano can increase feelings of calm. As with many of the other concepts discussed in this book, the more practiced this becomes, the easier it will be to achieve this, and the more powerful this becomes as a goal. Cleaning out the volcano allows room for reflection and emotional discharge, and this helps the body to produce and concentrate on producing calming chemical reactions. As people experience more calm, the better placed they will be to keep their volcanos from rumbling, and they'll reach for those icebergs less often.

Physical health benefits - When the volcano erupts, we know it has a significant impact on the body in terms of physical changes in the body and the release of chemicals and hormones. Therefore, repeated and consistent eruptions can have a lasting impact on the body, and we all know the problems that can be caused by ongoing experiences of stress. It can impact our hearts, and it can leave us feeling fatigued and exhausted. I'm not trying to suggest that children who lose their temper every now and again are on the cusp of a heart attack, but it is important to know that a lifetime of poor emotional management can have hugely negative impacts on health.

In summary, there are many benefits to keeping the volcano clean. In this chapter, we have covered some of these benefits and considered how they can encourage us to manage our volcanos better and how they can help us feel confident that we are doing something useful for our children. We've learned there are lots of good reasons to keep our volcanos clean, and this is what we need to bear in mind when we are talking to our children about these issues. In the next chapter, we are going to move things on and have a look at some of the techniques we can use to help us teach children how to process their emotions and clean their own volcanos out (with our support initially). So, what are you waiting for?

TWELVE
HOW TO CLEAN A VOLCANO

In the previous chapter, we spent some time considering why helping your child learn how to clean the volcano is a good idea, as well as some of the many benefits to ensuring that your child knows how to do this, and how it can help to improve their lives now and in the future. We know that if volcanos don't erupt, we can avoid explosive behaviour that leads to harmful consequences for a number of people. However, we also know that lava that has not been erupted out of the volcano is going to stay inside it, and it will potentially become slow-burning, damaging sludge that can build up and lead to other problems. It might even serve as a foundation for a future eruption, perhaps a complete overreaction to a relatively minor trigger.

What should we do instead? In this chapter, we'll focus on how to actually help your child clean out their volcano. This practice helps to teach the child about actually processing the emotion. They may have decided to manage it and avoided a harmful eruption. That's great, but they still have to do something with the lava. This processing of emotion and safely discharging it is the cleaning process that we are going to take a closer look at.

So, how do we go about helping our child to clean the volcano and learn these skills so they can practice them independently? There are a number of techniques that you can use to help your child learn how to express their emotions, so they can clean out the volcano of any sludge and are ready to move forward in terms of both the specific situation that triggered the volcano to rumble and their lives more generally. This book has been focused on the power of communication and emotional expression, and that theme continues here. The only real way that can reliably help children to process emotional experiences is for them to express it, and this volcano cleaning can occur in a number of different ways. Some of the most effective techniques for this are outlined below, but the general themes that apply to using all of them are similar.

Timing is important. There is no point trying to help your child empty the volcano until the rumbling is under control and a degree of calm and stability has been achieved. Once the icebergs have taken effect in a meaningful way, the volcano will be cool enough to be emptied. This is the time to approach your child and begin the process of cleaning the volcano. One of your main goals is to leave your child feeling rewarded and better as a result of expressing the emotion. If your child feels judged, criticised, or in any way looked down upon for expressing their emotions, you could inadvertently teach them that emotional expression is weak or is in some way wrong, and this can cause problems later on. We want the child to feel reassured and pleased that they decided to try to express themselves. They will then be much more likely to try this again in the future.

Talking - This is always going to be an option and, in some cases, is likely to be the most straightforward. As we have already established, children are all very different, and whilst some may find it too complicated or difficult to talk through their feelings, some will be able to do so in a perfectly straight-forward way. If they are good at expressing themselves verbally, ask your child how they felt. Try to establish what it was about the situation that they found so upsetting or so difficult to cope with at the time. Was it the words that were used by other people? Was it a sense of injustice? Perhaps they didn't fully understand what was being asked of them? Perhaps they were already in a bad mood, and they had not noticed quickly enough that the volcano was rumbling. Once you get your child used to talking about their emotions, you can start to help them notice patterns in the types of situations they find more difficult to keep their volcano cool.

Writing - Some children are not quite as good as others at explaining how they feel, and this can be for a variety of reasons. These children are still likely to be perfectly able to express their emotions; we just need to be more creative in how we help them do this. Some children, who are less able to express themselves verbally, might be able to do it through words. If they are at an age to write independently, perhaps give them a sheet to fill in with some of the questions that are suggested in the paragraphs above. They can then pass this to you when they feel the volcano is cooler, and you can still discuss it using the sheet as a prompt. Another advantage of this approach is that it gives the child more time to think things through. They might need a bit more time to process what happened and really make sense of what triggered the volcano in the first place.

Pictures - Your child might be quite artsy and, if so, you should take advantage of that skill and passion. If they enjoy the process of processing and expressing their emotions then this is even better. Perhaps they might like to draw a story board of what happened before, during, and after the volcano began to rumble or actually erupted. They might prefer a collage or just a simple drawing. As above, this image can then be used as a foundation for a conversation with you as the parent. Over time, the more approaches like this that are used the more the child will increase and improve their emotional vocabulary. This means that it won't be long before the images won't be needed any more, as they would have learned how to make sense of emotional events and talk about them with you.

Re-enactment - Have you got a little actor on your hands? Some people remember thoughts and feelings better when they're actually re-living the situation. Now, of course I'm not suggesting that you should make the actual situation happen again. Rather, you should ask your child to *walk and talk* their way through the situation. What happened when? Where were they standing/sitting? Where was the other person? What could they smell, see, and hear? Going through this process should help to trigger memories of what was actually difficult for your child to accept or understand, and this will help to uncover triggers and thoughts/feelings that your child may struggle to independently put into words.

Worry Eater - You might be wondering what a worry eater is. This is a useful tool that you can use with your child when you're going through the process of cleaning out the volcano. This technique might work better with slightly younger children and involves making a creature out of various boxes and bits and bobs from around the house. When you have used all the sticky-backed plastic you need, you will hopefully have a sweet but determined looking little critter (preferably with a letterbox style of mouth) that you can use to eat the worries expressed by your child. Once you have talked through whatever is on your child's mind, then you can write it down on a bit of paper (or draw it—whatever works best with your child's learning style), and post it into the mouth of the worry eater. The concept is straightforward. Once the worry eater has consumed the worry, then the child knows that the situation does not require any more of their attention.

Above are a number of techniques that you can use with your child to help them clean out their volcano. As with all of the skills and concepts covered in this book, the idea is that initially you will need to help your child through this process in a calm and patient way. Over time, your child will become able to use the skills a bit more automatically, without the need for as much support and intervention from yourself. You will always need to be available to listen of course—that part of the volcano cleaning process will always be your responsibility.

A central part of being someone who can really help clean out the volcano is knowing when is the best time to try to do this. Your child needs to be calm enough to talk through the situation without erupting all over again. So, look out for those rumbling clues. If you see them, postpone the cleaning process until the icebergs have fully melted. Your child may want to talk through the situation before they are really ready. If this is the case, gently help them understand that now may not be the best time for that. Also, as usual, there is a process of trial and error necessary here. Don't lose heart if one of the above suggestions does not work as well as you might have hoped, simply pick another and try again!

In this chapter, we have looked at a number of techniques that we can use to help our children clean the volcano. Remember that the key message in this chapter is that children are unlikely to know how to safely discharge and express their emotions, or how to *bounce back* from an eruption. As adults, part of our role is to help them learn and practice how to do this. There is no timeframe for this process. It could take a few weeks. It may take several months. Your child is learning a set of skills that will improve their lives and increase their chances of success in life significantly. Invest the time in this process and do not try to rush it. It is a process of trial and error, and you need to work as a team to help identify which techniques work the best for your child. It might be an arduous and emotionally testing process, but any positive results are invaluable.

SECTION IV:

MAINTAINING EMOTIONAL BALANCE

Chapters 13 – 18

THIRTEEN
EMOTIONAL INTELLIGENCE

In the previous chapter of this book, we have explored the actual icebergs—the nuts and bolts of how to help our children calm down and cool their volcanos. We have previously talked about why this is helpful, and why we should invest time in helping our children learn these skills. This chapter of the book is going to move on and consider another important set of issues —the concepts and the ways of understanding feelings that help us think more broadly about emotions. This is a useful foundation for some of the concepts that come later in this book. Firstly, we are going to cover the concept of emotional intelligence.

Emotional intelligence is the ability to recognise our own emotions, as well as the emotions of other people. Emotional intelligence also includes the ability to understand the differences between feelings, as well as appropriately label them (e.g. angry, sad, happy, afraid). The final element of emotional intelligence links to the ability to use emotional information to help guide our thinking and behaviour, as well as managing and adjusting the emotion to adapt to our environment and achieve our goals. You may know people who seem to be naturally skilled at either calming people down or helping to cheer them up—these are the emotional intelligence champions using their own skills in terms of emotional awareness and management to help other people regulate their feelings. Don't worry, you're on your way there too; using any of the techniques in this book with your child means you are improving and honing your skills as well. Your emotional intelligence will improve as you help your child improve theirs!

Emotional intelligence really came to the fore in the mid-1990s, and for many it was considered to be revolutionary, as it was viewed by some as the *missing link* in an unusual phenomenon that academics had struggled to explain rationally before that point. At that point in time, the experts knew that people with average levels of intelligence tended to outperform other people who had much higher levels of intelligence, which seemed illogical. Previously, it had always been assumed that IQ (the most commonly accepted measure of intelligence) was the central component in deciding the extent of someone's success. It then became clear that emotional intelligence was likely to be the attribute that helped people excel, and that in some way, this was more important than levels of general intelligence.

The concept of emotional intelligence is subject to some debate in academic circles, but I'm not going to drag you into all that! There is plenty to read on the topic online if you are interested, but for our purposes, I want to concentrate on how commonly accepted knowledge on the topic can help us.

So, why should we spend time thinking about emotional intelligence, and what are the benefits for us? Well, studies into the subject have shown that people who have a higher level of emotional intelligence are more likely to have greater levels of mental health, tend to perform better at work, have greater empathy skills, make better and more effective decisions, and have better levels of leadership skills. Another reported benefit from an increased level of emotional intelligence include having better social interactions, and this is particularly true for children and teenagers who have also demonstrated that improved emotional intelligence tends to reduce the chances of children engaging in anti-social behaviour and rule breaking. There is a link between increased levels of emotional intelligence and higher levels of academic achievement. This is different to levels of academic grades or qualifications, but it does support the idea that better emotional intelligence leads to more achievements.

These benefits also continue into adulthood, with the improved social relationships and the ability to *fit in* remaining present. Adults with improved emotional intelligence have a much better sense of their own emotional abilities and weaknesses, and this hugely reduces the chances of relational problems such as aggression and conflict. This also improves the perception that other people have of the emotionally intelligent individual—who wouldn't want to spend time with an empathic, pleasant, and understanding person so in tune with the emotions of themselves and other people? People with increased levels of emotional intelligence are much more likely to have better relationships with members of their family as well as intimate romantic partners. I think we all know a couple who seems to fight like cats and dogs. Perhaps, if they had a boost to their levels of emotional intelligence, there would be less need for the fighting, and they would understand their own and each other's emotions much more.

One of the more interesting relationships (in my humble opinion) is between emotional intelligence and negotiation skills. It has been suggested that the higher the level of emotional intelligence, the better the individual is at negotiating with others, as well as experiencing more improved work-based relationships more generally. In fact, it has been found that those with an increased level of emotional intelligence earn more on average than those with lower levels (not that money is everything of course—but it can be a nice bonus).

As stated above, having a higher level of emotional intelligence can lead to reduced chances of experiencing quite debilitating and generally negative situations, such as feelings of insecurity and depression. Having increased levels of emotional intelligence means people are more likely to have higher levels of life satisfaction and self-esteem, and they are much less likely to make poor health or other general choices. They are also more likely to enjoy the benefits of being able to manage stress more effectively and tend to be more resilient.

The great news for all of us is that just like other areas of our physical and mental abilities, we can improve our own levels of emotional intelligence. Much like with other abilities, we can think about emotional intelligence as a muscle; with exercise, we can make this muscle stronger and more effective. Without getting too technical about it, emotional intelligence relies on relationships and pathways being formed between the rational brain and the limbic system; therefore, effective communication between these two parts of the brain is crucial. Neurologists use the term *plasticity*, and this term describes the ability of the brain to change. As your brain changes, it develops new connections as new skills are learned. These changes are gradual, and as our brain cells develop new connections, these can speed up the efficiency of the new skills we are learning, such as emotional intelligence.

So, the more that you use the skills in this book, and the more you help your children learn, practice, and use these skills, then the more you will develop emotional intelligence in yourself and your child. These skills will equip them now, and they will also leave them much better placed to succeed in the future. The more you use and practice emotional intelligence related skills, the more habitual they will become; as with most things, practice makes perfect!

In this chapter, we have looked at the concept of emotional intelligence. This is our ability to process, understand, manage, and interact with our emotions in a productive and healthy way. This is a skill we can improve, and indeed we can help our children learn them, leading to increased chances of success for all!

FOURTEEN
HYPERMASCULINITY

In this chapter, we are going to have a closer look at the concept of hypermasculinity. You will probably not be too surprised to read that the focus of this chapter is going to be the boys. That's not to say that the issues covered in this chapter may very well apply to girls, but they are clearly much more likely to be relevant to male children. So, in this chapter, we are going to spend some time looking at what the concept of hypermasculinity actually is, how it manifests and what it might look like in children, and what the problems with it are. We will then spend some time focusing on how to manage, undermine, or prevent hypermasculinity being part of the lives of our sons, as well as how knowing about this issue helps to complement the rest of the tips and techniques that are covered in this book.

So, what is hypermasculinity? In simple terms, it is the word that is used to describe the presence of exaggerated male stereotypical behaviour. This includes a few elements, such as the affected individual placing emphasis on things such as physical strength, aggression, and sexuality. In other words, it's about that *macho* approach to life, which includes thinking that men need to be strong, and that this is how they should be perceived by the people around them. Men who experience hypermasculinity cannot bear the idea of being viewed as weak or feminine, or in any way having their manhood questioned or challenged. This, as you can imagine, can cause a number of varied and significant problems for these men and the people in their lives.

What does hypermasculinity look like? Well, it can manifest in a number of different ways. However, in terms of adult men, it can look like emotional indifference. It can make it difficult for men to accept love and display emotions that might leave them feeling more vulnerable, such as grief, fear, sadness, and shame. The responses this can lead to include rejection of others, isolation, silence, and withdrawal. A different response that it could contribute to is outright hostility and the acting out of anger. This is why anger is not always the most straightforward emotion to understand. It is often underpinned by other emotions that the individual is trying to protect or disguise. Men can often be inadvertently taught that to display anger is acceptable, even manly, but to show signs of being upset or scared is not acceptable. We call them macho, meatheads, jocks, and men's men, and they are likely to be unwitting victims of hypermasculinity.

One of the problems that research has indicated can be linked to the issue of hypermasculinity is physical and sexual violence towards women. Now, I need to insert a disclaimer here. I am not suggesting that any man who presents as being hypermasculine is going to commit physical and/or sexual harm towards a woman, but I am saying that this approach to life, and this way of thinking about themselves and other people in their lives, could leave them at increased vulnerability to behaving in negative ways towards women.

For the purposes of this book, one of the chief problems

associated with hypermasculinity that we are interested in is related to the impact it has on emotional management, emotional processing, and interactions with other people. One of the main elements of the concept of hypermasculinity is the belief that in order to demonstrate toughness, men should not display emotions, and should instead be emotionally hardened or indifferent. They should also be impassive at times of stress or intense emotion. The idea that this response to emotions demonstrates *character* is a key component of hypermasculinity. A psychologist specialising in sociology and emotions, Thomas J Scheff, has produced a lot of work on hypermasculinity, and is reported to have stated: '*It is masculine men that have* character. *A man with character who is under stress is not going to cry and blubber like a woman or child might.*' Essentially, the concept teaches that demonstrating emotions is a sign of weakness, and it is not something that is indulged in by 'real men.'

When adopted, this approach can lead to further problems in adult men. Firstly, it can encourage a process of self-imposed emotional monitoring, and it can be focused on ensuring that no emotions 'leak' out for fear of not retaining their position of power or strength. Some research (Ben-Zeev, Scharnetski, Chan & Dennehy, 2012) indicates that some men can actually actively avoid behaviours and attitudes such as compassion and emotional expression, as these traits are deemed to be feminine, and therefore need to be rejected and avoided. Scheff has added, '*The hypermasculine pattern leads to competition, rather than connection between persons.*' This means that in the context of intimate or emotional communication (especially confrontation) with women, the hypermasculine male often withdraws emotionally, refusing to engage in communication that might include emotional expression or discussion.

It is well known that men are at a higher risk of suicide than women, and that for men under 50, the biggest cause of death is suicide. Now, again, I'm not trying to suggest that if your son doesn't talk about their feelings they're going to kill themselves. I don't think it's a huge surprise that the group that society teaches should not talk about their feelings are the same group that are at the highest risk of suicide.

So, where does hypermasculinity come from? This is one of those hard to answer debates and, as always, there are a number of different theories that the academics continue to disagree about. For example, some argue that there is a link between the presence (or absence) of female hormones in women who are pregnant with boys, and that this is a significant contributory factor to the development of hypermasculinity. However, I think that there are probably a few key influences on the development of hypermasculinity in boys and that, as usually tends to be the case, it probably boils down to a few common-sense principles.

One of the explanations for the development of hypermasculinity in boys is the influence of the mainstream media. There are those that argue that images we see on television, advertisements, things we read in books, and messages passed through social media are responsible for telling boys that their job is to be strong, and that women require looking after. Therefore, one of the natural consequences of this approach is the idea that you should not let others see you as weak and that emotional expression is a sign of weakness. It is the classic 'boys don't cry' message. Have you ever seen James Bond, Superman, or Iron Man cry?

The idea of the strong man is everywhere in the media as well. We've all seen the adverts where the women swoon over the muscular man, where the man overcomes an adversary of some sort and gets the girl, or scenes where men are having to deal with overly emotional women who are allowing those dirty pesky feelings slip out and interrupt their day. These images and subliminal messages are bombarding us on a constant and daily basis, and they contribute to the reinforcement in our society (of course how deliberate this is, is subject to much debate that we do not have the time or space for here). As these messages are also going to be present in magazines aimed at young men and teenagers, it is not difficult to see why emotional intelligence, and the ability to openly share the process of emotional expression is so lacking in boys.

The main difficulty with all of this though is that not only are our male children being conditioned into not allowing emotions to be part of their lives, but we inadvertently reinforce this. How often have you heard someone you know telling someone in their life to 'man up.' That is hardly a helpful message to be installing! Some mothers will often make statements such as 'Well, boys will be boys,' or 'You know what boys are like.' These simply serve to reinforce and support the idea that emotions are not for the boys. It is also likely to reduce the motivation of these mothers to be comfortable with allowing their boys to cry or to encourage them to talk about how they're feeling. Have they not got just as much right as their sister to feel upset or scared when pinched or shouted at by another child?

The bad news is that it is probably not possible to protect your son from all messages about hypermasculinity and 'how to be a man.' The good news is that some of the most powerful and meaningful messages they get about this are from their parents. So, your job is to help them understand that it is okay for them to be upset, to have feelings, and to talk about those feelings. It's a tricky thing to do. You'll need to reinforce positive messages about emotional management and intelligence, and also try to counteract the negative messages about this coming from everywhere else!

Hypermasculinity is a pressing issue in society today. It

won't stop being an issue unless we teach our boys that emotions are not to be feared or swallowed. Part of our role as guardians of boys is to help them learn and develop emotional intelligence. If they come to view emotional intelligence, particularly emotional expression, as a sign of strength rather than weakness, we will be helping future generations more generally as well as our children specifically. Volcanos need to let off steam gradually, and they need to know that it is okay for them to do that. Let's get to work helping them understand why it is not only okay but essential to their long-term futures.

FIFTEEN

EFFECTIVE MODELLING: HOW IS YOUR VOLCANO?

In this chapter, we're going to shift our attention slightly. Up to this point, we've been very focused on how your children manage their volcanos. Now I want you to spend some time thinking about your own volcano. 'Why are you asking us to do that,' I hear you cry! Well, we've talked quite a lot about your role as parents and guardians and how you can have a huge impact on how your children manage and cope with their volcano. You can do this in a very obvious way by teaching them the material in this book.

However, there is another much more subtle and harder-to-detect way that you teach your children about emotions—simply by being yourself. We all know that children are like sponges when they're born, soaking up all of the information and feedback they get from the world around them. In the early years of life, before the friends take over, the most important influences in a child's life are their parents/guardians. This means that you can sometimes inadvertently teach them all sorts of things when you don't even realise that it is happening.

This is why it is so important to keep control of your own

volcano, and this is what we are going to cover in this chapter. Imagine all of your hard work being undone by a few unguarded moments when you react less helpfully or you yourself completely lose the plot. Children do not cope well with mixed messages, so these adult slips can negatively impact on all of the valuable emotional intelligence you've been helping them develop.

Now, I don't want you to panic. I am not for one moment suggesting that you have to be a paragon of virtue who never makes a mistake and is absolutely masterful in terms of emotional management. But, what I am saying is that you will need to do your best to practice what you preach and show your child that you yourself also use icebergs when the volcano is rumbling, and that these skills are worth investing the time and effort in. Children are not going to value things if we undermine them by not doing it as we say. The whole 'Don't do as I do, do as I say,' is fairly nonsensical and works against learning logic. Children learn by watching, so try to make sure they are watching the right thing.

The above is important, but that does not equate to it being easy. Children themselves can bring out the best and worst in us as parents. There are those times (most days in my case) where we feel stressed, tired, overworked, underpaid, and then we are faced with a trigger that starts heating up our own volcano. It can be difficult for us to stay on top of our own feelings. In order to stay calm, you could, of course, use any of the icebergs that you have helped your child learn about, although you can modify them to be more adult friendly. It might be worth keeping a diary of the times when you felt you did not manage your feelings very well. What happened before you began to lose control? These are the triggers and before long you should start to see patterns in the triggers. These will help you notice them earlier so you can take steps to avoid the eruption!

We have discussed encouraging your child to make sure the volcano is cool before they try to clean it out. The same applies to you. If your child was part of the trigger, explain to them that you will need to discuss what happened soon, but not right now, and that you are taking some time to cool down. Hopefully, this will help the child to understand that their behaviour has not gone unnoticed, and that there will be consequences (if necessary). Something that is really important, can be really empowering, and can act as an important bonding experience is to apologise on the occasions when you are wrong, or times when you did not try to cool your volcano appropriately. This teaches children that it is okay to make mistakes, and that we all do, as well as reinforcing the need to make amends through apology.

Finally, you need to be kind to yourself. You are but a simple human, and you won't get everything right. We need to help our children navigate through the challenging process of improving emotional intelligence, and that also applies to ourselves. Forgive yourself when things go a bit wonky, this is going to happen, and as long as you try not to repeat the same mistakes then the chances of you doing significant damage are likely to be slim. Don't forget to celebrate success. If your child is doing well, tell them, and give yourself a pat on the back—you've had a role in that!

So, in this chapter we have discussed the issue of modelling. Children watch our every move. Even when we think they're not paying attention to us, they're still soaking up all of the obvious and subtly subconscious messages that we are passing on. This is why the approach to emotional management discussed in this book is not a fad and should not be treated as such. It is a lifestyle choice that you need to commit to, and you need to be invested in it as much as possible. Think of it as something that you should be using even if nobody is watching. That's the best way to help it become a habit for both you and your children. When they see that you as their parents buy into and value the approach, they will too. And by the time that your influence has worn a little thinner, the skills will be ingrained, and they will have the habits that we have covered in this book so far that will greatly increase their chances of success in life.

SIXTEEN
TRIGGERS AND PATTERNS

In this chapter, we're going to spend some time looking at the concepts of triggers and patterns. These are important issues, as once these are ingrained in your mind, you can begin to pre-empt difficult situations and be able to take aversive action when necessary. This also means that you can prepare your child for these difficult trigger-filled situations, which will leave them better placed to be ready to use some icebergs if necessary. Knowledge is power, and this knowledge can be crucial in helping children to stay in charge of their emotions and avoid eruptions.

So, what do we mean when we refer to triggers then? A trigger, as I will be talking about it in this chapter, refers to anything that can start the volcano rumbling. Triggers can take many different forms, and they tend to fall into two categories: internal and external. Internal triggers are things that come from within us. This might be our memories, our physical health, or our senses. External triggers, as you may have already guessed, relate to things that are outside of ourselves. This can include places, other people, situations, and certain times of the day.

As adults, we know the kinds of situations that are likely to get our volcanos rumbling. Whether it is waiting in a post office queue whilst someone takes an inordinately long amount of time to get themselves organised, or being stuck behind another car in which the driver is crawling along in a national speed limit part of the road, we all have our individual pet peeves. Think about the things in your life that drive you potty. What is it that will get you from nought to sixty in three seconds? These are good examples of what we would call triggers.

Other examples might include being 'hangry,' which is effectively being very irritable when hungry. This is a classic trigger for me, and I do not cope well with hunger. Some people struggle to contain their emotions during certain times of the day or in response to certain stimulus. Think about your own children. What are the types of situations when they tend to struggle to keep the volcano cool? Perhaps it's the struggle in an environment where there is a lot of noise? Perhaps the volcano is quite vulnerable to erupting when your child is in a situation where there are a lot of new people they don't know? Maybe they don't cope as well later in the day or at times they are being asked to complete certain tasks?

I've asked you to do a fair amount of thinking above and you may be wondering why. Well, there are clear advantages to having a good level of awareness about what can get the volcano rumbling. Once you have an understanding of what the patterns are in your child's volcano rumbling, you will know what to look out for. If you know that your child does not manage their volcano particularly well when they are hot, and they are due to go to the beach with school or friends, then you can prepare them and help them understand that they need to be extra vigilant to any rumblings and that they may need to have some icebergs ready to deploy once they notice those early rumbles.

Identifying and understanding the patterns of the triggers that can cause a volcano to start rumbling is really important. This knowledge is central to early detection of volcano rumbling. If you know that a commonly problematic trigger is on the horizon, you are ahead of the game and poised to help intervene when necessary. Spotting the triggers is a great habit to pass on to your children too. This is part of emotional intelligence, as we discussed in Chapter 13, and it will help your child in terms of their emotional management skills.

So, how do we learn what the relevant triggers to volcano rumblings are? Well, the most obvious technique is good old-fashioned observation. If you were able to answer the questions above, you may have been surprised at what you already know about the triggers that can be difficult for your child to cope with. Remember, as someone who spends a lot of time with your child, it is unlikely that these regular disturbances will go unnoticed.

However, don't panic or beat yourself up if you feel like you're not sure about what these triggers are. You are unlikely to be the only adult in your child's life. What have other adults noticed about your child? What kinds of situations do they see the volcano rumbling in? Again, teachers are a good source of information here. They see your child for a long time every day and often in situations where they may be more vulnerable to experiencing triggers. Therefore, they will be an excellent source of information for you. Another option is to keep a journal. Perhaps jot down a few notes at points your child's volcano erupts, or comes close to eruption. What was happening just before the volcano started to rumble? What could you see or hear (presuming you were there)? What can your child tell you about what pushed them over the edge? Keeping a journal like this for a few weeks will help you to develop an understanding of what acts as triggers for your child.

In this chapter, we have looked at triggers to the volcano rumbling and what the patterns of these triggers can tell us. If you can spot these patterns, and develop a solid understanding of the triggers that can cause problems for your child, then you can help them put things in place to break the chain and prevent the volcano from erupting, and maybe even from rumbling at all. This knowledge will complement the emotional intelligence that your child is developing, and with your support, they can move that one step closer to mastery over their emotions.

SEVENTEEN
RELAXATION AND MINDFULNESS

In this chapter, we will spend some time looking at a couple of techniques that can be really helpful in keeping volcanos cool and under control in the long term. These techniques are relaxation and mindfulness, and they are relatively easy to do and have the added bonus of being completely free! We're investing some time in exploring these issues in this chapter as often prevention is better than a cure, an expression that I'm sure you have heard before. The premise is that rather than waiting for the volcano to erupt and then having to use an iceberg, we can use these techniques to keep the volcano nice and cool, so that it takes longer to begin to rumble, and hopefully the chances of an eruptions are greatly reduced.

Relaxation is quite a broad term, and it can be achieved through a number of different means. One of the approaches that I find to be particularly helpful is called PMR (progressive muscle relaxation). This is a very simple technique that involves lying down (or sitting in a comfortable chair) and taking each muscle in turn, tensing and relaxing. So, you might start with your toes by stretching them as much as you can, before relaxing them for a set number of seconds. This contrast between tensing and relaxing is quite noticeable and encourages you to observe the more relaxing feelings that arise when your body is in a state of rest.

Mindfulness is a very trendy topic at the moment, and I can see why. There are many books on the topic, some of which are excellent, so I will not dive down into the details here. It can be considered a form of meditation, but the difference is a very clear focus on not becoming caught up in your own thinking, which we know can be a great source of stress if we are not careful. Mindfulness helps us to see and accept things as they are and we can achieve a sense of peace with the fact that things around us change and that things are not always as we would like them to be. It can help us cope with the ups and down of life and be more aware of ourselves and other people around us. Most importantly, the main goals also include feeling safe, calm, and peaceful, as well as being more accepting and understanding of ourselves and others.

Using mindfulness involves being quiet and sitting comfortably. You can close your eyes if you want, but it is not essential. A good alternative is to choose a point on the wall or floor to focus your eyes on if you don't wish to close them. Once you are positioned comfortably, you can begin the process, which is ultimately aimed at clearing your mind and focusing on the moment, which can be really important in re-centring yourself and your brain, which is a complicated piece of kit often processing a huge number of operations simultaneously. Mindfulness involves paying attention and 'tuning in' to what is going on around you, as well as what you are thinking and feeling. It is focused on being in the present moment, being aware of things as they are now, and clearing your mind of everything else. It is important that you give yourself time whilst you are doing this, and that you try to avoid responding automatically to any thoughts and feelings that may arise. Also, let go of any judgement about yourself and others; a core component of mindfulness is maintaining an openhearted and kind approach.

The above techniques will not work for everyone, it's important that I offer that disclaimer at this point. You may have other relaxation techniques that work for you, whether that be a round of golf, going for a run, curling up with a good book, or going for a walk. The key message here is that, as a parent, you need to ensure that you are investing time in keeping your own volcano cool. It is all well and good helping your children increase their emotional intelligence, but even us parents can learn a thing or two about this. The famous analogy is about being on an aeroplane and putting on your own oxygen mask before helping your children with theirs. It makes a lot of sense. It will be much easier for you to help your children keep their volcanos cool if yours is nicely maintained—much better than a set of chain reactions and multiple eruptions all over the place!

The above techniques can be done with your little volcanos. They may need a bit more time to get used to relaxation techniques, and they may need to practice them a little more, but there is no reason that they cannot also benefit. You could do them together, which will also have the benefits of offering a bonding opportunity for you all. And don't forget one of my favourite aspects of these techniques—a lot of them are free! In a world where everything seems to cost money, a free opportunity to improve life and achieve some inner peace sounds good to me.

We've covered some basic relaxation and mindfulness techniques in this chapter. There are many ways to relax, and I am not going to be able to list them all here. Ultimately, you know yourself best, and you will know what kinds of activities can help you to relax. Don't feel guilty about this or feel that it is a self-indulgence. It is not. In fact, it is a really important part of maintaining a cool volcano, and ultimately, a happy and peaceful home. You may have read this chapter and feel very sceptical about the suggestions that have been made. I'm not offended and was very sceptical myself before I tried. They have made a big difference to my life and could well benefit you too. As they are free, there is nothing to lose, so I would encourage you to try them and make your own mind up.

EIGHTEEN
FEEDBACK AND REINFORCEMENT

In this chapter, we will cover the issues of feedback and reinforcement and how they can contribute to maintaining a cool and calm volcano. We will spend some time considering how these processes work, how to make the most of the benefits that can be achieved through them, and how these benefits can greatly increase the chances of peace being maintained.

Let's start with the concept of feedback. This is probably a term you're familiar with, and this is the process of receiving information about the way that you have completed a particular task. Similarly, as well as receiving feedback, we can provide other people with feedback about how they have done. This is where it comes into play in terms of helping children improve their emotional management skills. Once children have a handle on the basics of using icebergs to cool the volcano, the focus can shift to tweaking the way in which they use the skills. This means that when you're talking things through with your child, you can give them a bit of feedback about what you saw. What bits of the process did you think they did particularly well? What did they find difficult? What might they need to think about trying to do differently the next time?

It might be that you need to give your child some constructive feedback about what they did. This can feel quite difficult, especially if you can see that they are really trying but perhaps are not quite achieving what they would like. At these times, it is really important not to dishearten your child. Always start with some positive feedback, and even if things have gone spectacularly wrong, always start with something positive that you can praise. This will increase the chances of the child remaining motivated to try to use the techniques. Try to be gentle and sensitive when pointing out the parts of the process that did not work very well. It can often be helpful to think about examples of times you yourself have been learning new skills and struggled; this will help your child understand that it is a process of learning that will take a period of time to learn and master.

Feedback is important as it helps you child to learn what parts of the process they are succeeding at and which parts they need to pay more attention to. This directs their learning and encourages them to become more reflective in how they think about how they have done in managing their emotions. After a while, don't be surprised if you don't really need to give you child feedback. They are likely to be able to spot themselves what worked well and what did not go as well. This is another indication of their own developing awareness, as well as their progress in terms of improving their emotional intelligence more generally.

Reinforcement is a broad concept that I will not go into huge amounts of detail here, as whole books have been written on the topic. In simple terms, what you need to know is that reinforcement can be both positive and negative, and it can encourage or discourage us from doing certain things. Think about trying to lose weight. There is a reason that often it is easier to do this if you are attending a weight loss group rather than doing it on your own. This is because if you are doing it with others, you get constant positive reinforcement and support from the other members of the group. This mutual positive reinforcement is what keeps people going and helps them say no to that cheeky biscuit or that second portion of dinner. This can be applied to any activity including emotional management.

Feedback is a form of reinforcement. Over time, you give your child positive reinforcement and praise for the efforts they have made at keeping the volcano cool and the successes they have achieved on this front. This positive reinforcement strengthens their motivation to carry on trying. On the flip side, if you provide your child with negative reinforcement, or insensitive negative feedback, then you may inadvertently put your child off from trying to manage their emotions, which is why providing feedback sensitively and carefully is so crucial.

As we've established, learning emotional management skills and keeping the volcano cool can be a challenging process. Therefore, your child may need some extra motivation or inducements to try to keep the volcano cool, at least until they start doing it and seeing the benefits for themselves. You might set up an agreement whereby every five times your child manages to cool the volcano they receive some kind of treat. Of course, you will need to be careful that you are not encouraging your child to create situations where they need to calm down. You will know best what types of treats or encouragement will work with your child.

In summary, positive feedback and reinforcement are important tools in the process of helping children improve their emotional intelligence. Once you have a way of using these tools effectively, you have the power to encourage your child to keep trying to cool the volcano, even at times when they may be struggling to use these skills or when they are becoming disheartened with the process.

NEXT STEPS

At the start of this book, I made you a promise.

I promised that if you followed the advice and suggestions in this book, you would be in a position to help your child feel calmer, manage their anger, and increase the levels of peace and harmony in your family home. I promised that you'd be able to do it for free, and that it could lead to many benefits and a closer bond between you and the little volcanos in your life.

One of the key parts of the promise was that you needed to follow the guidelines and suggestions made in this book.

I'm not going to lie to you and suggest that helping children learn how to improve their emotional management skills is easy, or that this book is a magic wand. However, following the guidelines offered here will be a great start on your journey to helping your child improve their emotional intelligence.

I stand by my promise. I am confident that the material in this book can make a big difference in your life and the lives of your family, especially the little volcanos you share your life with.

What are you waiting for? It's time to get started!

FREE PRINTABLE POSTER TO HELP COOL THE VOLCANO!

This book has covered a range of techniques, called icebergs, which can help your child to learn how to manage their emotions and become more emotionally intelligent.

These techniques are now available to you in the form of a free printable poster, which you can access by clicking the following link below:

https://mailchi.mp/e0abdcb7ded5/ctv

Please download the poster, print it out, and put it on a wall where your little volcano can see it, and you can use it together!

Thank you for reading my book. If you enjoyed it, you can make a big difference.

Reviews are the most powerful tools in my arsenal when it comes to getting attention for my books. Much as I'd like to, I don't have the financial muscle of a New York or London publisher. I can't take out full page ads in the newspaper or put posters on the subway.

But I'd like to think I have something more powerful land effective than that, and it is something that most writers would love to get their hands on.

A kind and helpful bunch of readers.

I really appreciate all of your feedback, and I love hearing what you have to say. I need your input to make the next version better, and to help my career as a writer. Honest reviews of my books help bring them to the attention of other readers they could help.

If you've enjoyed this book or found it helpful, I would be very grateful if you could spend just five minutes leaving a review (it can be as short as you like) on the book's Amazon page. You can jump right to the page by clicking below:

UK

US

Also, please feel free to email me your thoughts: petecblack@gmail.com

Thank you so much!

Peter Black

ISBN-10: 1986036111
ISBN-13: 978-1986036115

I am on Facebook – https://www. facebook.com/peterblackwriter

I am on Twitter - @petecblack
Please check out my website – www.petercblack.co.uk

Printed in Great Britain
by Amazon

45740828R00066